THE
WIT
AND
WISDOM
OF
REALITY
TV

THE WIT AND WISDOM OF REALITY TV

by A. Housemate

ORION

First published in hardback in Great Britain in 2005 by
Orion Books
an imprint of the Orion Publishing Group Ltd
Orion House, 5 Upper St Martin's Lane,
London WC2H 9EA

10 9 8 7 6 5 4 3 2 1

A CIP catalogue record for this book is available
from the British Library.

ISBN: 0 75287 518 3

Illustrations by Mr Bingo www.mr-bingo.com

Printed and bound by Mackays of Chatham, Kent plc

Every effort has been made to fulfil requirements with regard to
reproducing copyright material. The publisher will be glad to rectify
any omissions at the earliest opportunity.

www.orionbooks.co.uk

To the producers and programme planners who have constipated our screens with reality TV shows, I salute you.

Keep them coming ... we all love a laugh.

TOP 25 INSULTS ON REALITY TV

@!#*!

INSULT NUMBER 25

'Janet Street-Porter was perhaps one of the scariest creatures I encountered in the jungle.'

PAUL BURRELL, *I'm a Celebrity ... Get Me Out of Here!,* Series 4

Why ARE You on My TV?

'Now, who in their right frame of mind would make themself look like a doughnut on purpose?' JADE, *BB3*

'I'm occasionally funny, occasionally annoying and I've got great tits.' ABI TITMUSS, *Celebrity Love Island*

'I have a great big ego.' HUGGY BEAR, *I'm a Celebrity . . . Get Me Out of Here!*, Series 4

'My band will be star-struck, man! You're A-list. I'm not even *on* a list.' KENZIE, on introducing BRIGITTE NIELSEN to Blazin' Squad, *Celebrity Big Brother*, Series 3

CLAUDE LITTNER [interviewing SAIRA for the job]: 'You refer to yourself as somebody who is impulsive, impatient, unreasonable, stubborn, confrontational. Now, to an employer that is a red rag.'
SAIRA: 'I don't think they're negative skills.'
The Apprentice

'The reason is because I'm a masochistic freak.' NATALIE APPLETON, on appearing on reality TV, *I'm a Celebrity … Get Me Out of Here!*, Series 4

'In medieval times I would have been called Sir Hump-A-Lot.' VICTOR, *BB5*

'Basically obviously you know I'm a great fan of yours you know and … and you know your shows and stuff and but … what roughly you know what you do and you know and basically how … how you obviously you used to DJ and you know and you've moved into hypnotism you know hypnosis type of thing why you know what made you take that on full time 'cos it looks like it's a fairly full-time task now?' RAJ to PAUL McKENNA, *The Apprentice*

'I'm here because I can be entertaining and a pain in the arse.' PAUL DANAN, *Celebrity Love Island*

'I can fit a four-finger Kit Kat in my mouth that way [sideways].' JADE, *BB3*

INSULT
NUMBER 24

'The problem is you have the personality of two fleas.'

SIMON COWELL, *The X Factor,*
Series 1

General Knowledge

'You see those things . . . don't think I'm being daft . . . but them things that look like eyes, are they their real eyes?' JADE on peacocks, *BB3*

'What is the official title of the Queen's husband?'

'Prince Philip of England?' ABI TITMUSS, *Celebrity Love Island*

BRIAN: 'What if she's [Helen] got an IQ of twenty-five?'
HELEN: 'Actually, I'm only twenty-three.' *BB2*

'What is the currency of Japan?'

'It's only in Europe where they do euros, right? Dollars.' LADY ISABELLA HERVEY, *Celebrity Love Island*

'What does "diabolical" mean in England?'
JACKIE STALLONE, *Celebrity Big Brother*,
Series 3

'Can I stop you? Mary Poppins is not real.'
ALEX, *BB3*

'Who composed Beethoven's 5th Symphony?'

'Umm … Err …' LADY ISABELLA HERVEY, *Celebrity Love Island*

'Jimmy, isn't that the name of a baby kangaroo?' HELEN, *BB2*

'Spell "celebrity".'

'Err …' CALLUM BEST, *Celebrity Love Island*

'I can't sleep, I think you've given me that disease, Jonny, insomnina.' JADE, *BB3*

'What is the square root of thirty-six?'

'Nine.' PAUL DANAN, *Celebrity Love Island*

'Five and twenty years … how long is that?' TIM, *BB3*

'Do you know if you put hot water in the kettle it boils quicker?' SPENCER, *BB3*

'What's Chiblial Pursuit? I don't know what you're talking about.' JADE, when asked to play Trivial Pursuit, *BB3*

'What is eight times nine?'

'Seventy . . . nine?' REBECCA LOOS, *Celebrity Love Island*

'You know Jack Daniels . . . he does all the magic stuff!' HELEN, *BB2*

'They do speak English there, don't they?' JADE about the USA, *BB3*

And the best *Big Brother* conversation ever . . .

SPENCER: 'You know you see those people in Venice standing on the back of gondolas, pushing it around?'

JADE: 'They don't do that on the Thames though, do they?'

SPENCER: 'No. I don't work on the Thames. I work in Cambridge.'

JADE: 'Is there not the Thames there?'

SPENCER: 'No!'

JADE: 'Is there a river called the Cambridge river?'

SPENCER: 'Yeah, it's called the Cam.'

JADE: 'Really? You swear? I only thought there was the Thames. I thought that was the main one in London.'

SPENCER: 'It is. I don't live in London.'

JADE: 'I'm confused. I thought Cambridge was in London. I knew Birmingham weren't in London.'

SPENCER: 'Would you like to go and tell the group what you just said?'

JADE: 'No . . .'

SPENCER: 'Cambridge is a city.'

JADE: 'But we've got a city in London.'

SPENCER: 'Yes. This city is called London. And there's different parts of it. Cambridge is a city.'

JADE: 'Of where? Kent? Well, England's a country, London's a city, Bermondsey's just a throw-off. Now where are you? What's your country, and what's your things?'

SPENCER: 'What country am I from? England. The city is called Cambridge, the county Cambridgeshire.'

JADE: 'So not Kent, then?'

SPENCER: 'Nooooo . . . The region is called East Anglia.'

JADE: 'Where's East Angular, though? I thought that was abroad.'

SPENCER: 'Jade, have you been taking the stupid pills again?'

JADE: 'Every time people tell me they work in East Angular, I actually think they're talking about near Tunisia and places like that. Am I thick?'

SPENCER: 'Well, I hate to say it, but you are.'

JADE: "Cos Scottish and Irish and all that comes under England, doesn't it?'

SPENCER: 'No . . . They come under Great Britain. Scotland and Wales have their own flags. Northern Ireland and Ireland are different.'

JADE: 'So they're not together? Where's Berlin?'

SPENCER: 'Germany . . .' *BB3*

INSULT NUMBER 23

'Edwina's like the granny that won't die.'

GORDON RAMSAY, *Hell's Kitchen,*
Series I

It's OK, I'm a Celebrity . . .

'Various people who appear on this show have been accused of playing up to the cameras, showing off and trying to appeal to the viewers at any cost ... All we've got to say about that is it's our job and we're very sorry.'
ANT and DEC, fronting *I'm a Celebrity ... Get Me Out of Here!*

'We're gonna be OK. We've got lip gloss.'
NUSH, *BB4*

'My brother showed me her on the internet and now she's in there moaning like something out of *One Flew Over*.' PAUL DANAN on ABI TITMUSS, *Celebrity Love Island*

'I joined the show because I can't get a record deal and when 17 million people a day are watching you, the record companies are more interested.' BRIAN HARVEY, *I'm a Celebrity ... Get Me Out of Here!*, Series 4

RICHIE NEVILLE: 'So what do you actually do, Rebecca?'
REBECCA LOOS: 'Nothing.' *The Farm*, Series 1

'I've never been stalked. It doesn't happen in Wales.' HELEN, *BB2*

'This is worse than a boxing match. In a boxing match it's over by the fourth round. I've had 200 rounds in here.' NIGEL BENN, *I'm a Celebrity ... Get Me Out of Here!*, Series 1

'I know I'll have arrived when I have my own dishwasher.' JON, *BB4*

'The kitchen is full of dishes. Who will clean them?' JACKIE STALLONE, *Celebrity Big Brother*, Series 3

'I hate reality TV.' MICHAEL GRECO, *Celebrity Love Island*

'Can I work for Playboy TV?' LEE, *BB3*

'They should send in champagne. We have survived that creature.' JOHN McCRIRICK on JACKIE STALLONE, *Celebrity Big Brother*, Series 3

'I hate reality shows like *Big Brother* and *I'm a Celebrity*. I'd rather watch a goldfish bowl.' JANET STREET-PORTER, *I'm a Celebrity … Get Me Out of Here!*, Series 4

'They are going to work us so hard it's going to be a personal test because I've never done a decent day's work in my life.' AL MURRAY, *Celebrity Hell's Kitchen*

'In my eyes I did not kiss and tell.' REBECCA LOOS, *Celebrity Love Island*

'I just want to stay at home, sleep late and go to lunch, over and over again.' TANIA, *BB4*

'As far as I was concerned, it was going to be like *Ibiza Uncovered* with dodgy sexual games, but it's been nothing like that.' LEE SHARPE, *Celebrity Love Island*

'I've been in the business for twenty years, then I come on this show, sit on my arse, eat crap and jump out of an aeroplane and now everyone wants to talk to me. It's amazing.' JOE PASQUALE, *I'm a Celebrity ... Get Me Out of Here!*, Series 4

'Who the fuck does she think she is? A girl with a pair of plastic boobs ... I have seen another side. She just thinks I'm some ex-soap star.' PAUL DANAN on ABI TITMUSS, *Celebrity Love Island*

'You're making a fool of me now.' PAUL DANAN, *Celebrity Love Island*

'Today I was just a zombie. I was just lying around.' LADY VICTORIA HERVEY, *The Farm*, Series 1

'How old were you when you decided to take all your clothes off?' URI GELLER to NELL McANDREW, *I'm a Celebrity ... Get Me Out of Here!*, Series 1

'Do you know who I am? ... Well you should do. If you read *Tatler* you would. But judging by your clothes, it's obvious you don't.' JASMINE LENNARD, *Trust Me, I'm a Holiday Rep*

'I'll miss my AA meetings.' SOPHIE ANDERTON, *I'm a Celebrity ... Get Me Out of Here!*, Series 4

'You think I came 10,000 miles for this? I've never suffered so much in my life!' JACKIE STALLONE, on having a meal without wine, *Celebrity Big Brother*, Series 3

'They've hidden my make-up bag. I want to leave.' SAM, *BB6*

'I can't remember a night I enjoyed less in my entire life. I woke up this morning and for the first time was thinking, I really don't want to live today.' AMANDA BARRIE, *Hell's Kitchen*, Series 1

'I'm a rap star; I'm not a sheep herder.' VANILLA ICE, *The Farm*, Series 1

'Can't face not seeing myself.' TONY BLACKBURN when asked why he'd taken a mirror to the jungle as a luxury item, *I'm a Celebrity . . . Get Me Out of Here!*, Series 1

'If I don't disappear before your very eyes, I despair, really.' VANESSA FELTZ, *Celebrity Fit Club*, Series 2

'I watched *Celebrity Love Island* because Jonathan Ross said that Abi Titmuss and Rebecca Loos were crying. But when I turned it on they were having a good time so I turned it off. They weren't in agony. They weren't getting hurt. Think if the rest of the world got wiped out and humanity had to start again with that lot. You'd be left with a bunch of ropey old sluts and desperate wannabes.' RICKY GERVAIS on *Celebrity Love Island*

INSULT
NUMBER 22

'Whatever, wannabe, loser, jealous, you know it! Sex-u-al.'

CRAIG, *BB6*

On Friendship . . .

'The odds are we are all going to kill each other.' JOHN LYDON, *I'm a Celebrity . . . Get Me Out of Here!*, Series 3

'If we've got a gang, it's pretty short on numbers, we need to get recruiting.' ALEX, *BB3*

'If one of me mates got into bed with us, I'd probably get him in a headlock.' ANTHONY, *BB6*

'I've had better days. We didn't get along, had no laughs, we had no cocktails. At one point we were like Del Boy and Rodders, and the best bit was when Michael gave me a piece of his chewed orange peel.' ABI TITMUSS on MICHAEL GRECO, *Celebrity Love Island*

'Look at me! Anthony! Look at me! I am Craig! I am your best friend ... Anthony ... I am your best friend within this house ... Anthony, are you all right?' CRAIG, *BB6*

'Let's have more mundane conversations.' VIC REEVES, *I'm a Celebrity ... Get Me Out of Here!*, Series 4

'I'd like Jon if he stopped nagging me.' NUSH, *BB4*

'We'll call you Lucy Lovelips, and I'm Leroy. Leroy Love.' JONNY to KATE, *BB3*

'The thing is, I won't go into too much detail, but I've hung out with Abi before the show but I haven't spent a lot of time with her on a daytime, sober level.' CALLUM BEST, *Celebrity Love Island*

'I love Callum very much, we have chemistry, but you two have chemistry and you have my blessing. I mean that, but can I watch?' ABI TITMUSS to REBECCA LOOS, *Celebrity Love Island*

'There's just too much love in the room.' FEDERICO, *BB4*

'Let me tell you something right now, the red team are not there to wipe your arse and you've run out of fucking risotto rice, sweetheart.' GORDON RAMSAY to EDWINA CURRIE, *Hell's Kitchen*, Series 1

'She's funny, quirky and she doesn't think she is the poodle's doodles!' MICHAEL GRECO on ABI TITMUSS, *Celebrity Love Island*

'For fuck's sake, I've got Jade on my team, I won't get anywhere!' ALEX, *BB3*

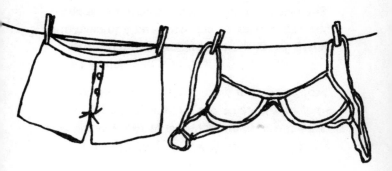

'I'm going to be in the Love Shack with some psycho yoga bitch, levitating across my bed in the night like *Ghostbusters*.' FRAN COSGROVE on sharing the Love Shack with JAYNE MIDDLEMISS, *Celebrity Love Island*

'I do not want your comfort!' AHMED to MARCO, *BB5*

'It's a bit harsh to blame Paul but I will.' JAMES, *The Apprentice*

'She was the most fucking decent girl in here. She had morals ... she was always pushing me away.' JASON on VANESSA, *BB5*

'Stop snoring and stop farting because you are smelling the place out.' MICHAEL GRECO reading out an anonymous letter from the cast addressed to him, *Celebrity Love Island*

'I can't believe how much support I've had over the years from Tom Hanks.' PAUL BURRELL, *I'm a Celebrity ... Get Me Out of Here!*, Series 4

'I thought, who gave Barbie coffee? It was like talking, talking, just noise and not saying anything.' JAYNE MIDDLEMISS on NIKKI ZIERING, *Celebrity Love Island*

INSULT NUMBER 21

'Tweedle Dee, Tweedle Dum and Tweedle Twat.'

SCIENCE on ANTHONY, CRAIG and MAXWELL, *BB6*

On Psychology . . .

'She's about as stable as Rik Waller jumping up and down on a three-legged table.' VICTOR on KITTEN, *BB5*

'Somewhere inside my heart I knew I would go first – this was a psychic feeling.' URI GELLER, *I'm a Celebrity . . . Get Me Out of Here!*, Series 1

'What these little cats don't know is there are some jungle cats in here playing the game.' JASON, *BB5*

'I'm not normal – normality sucks. I'm a freak and I love it.' JAYNE MIDDLEMISS, *Celebrity Love Island*

'When you wake up in the morning and the first thing you hear is some bloke saying, "Oh God, where have I put my stilettos?" you know you're in the nuthouse.'
MAXWELL, *BB6*

'Can I just say something? Is Janet moody?'
BRIAN HARVEY, *I'm a Celebrity ... Get Me Out of Here!*, Series 4

'To be the man you got to beat the man. And I am the man.' VICTOR, *BB5*

'You're barking mad, dear. Completely fucking barking mad!' DEREK on KINGA, *BB6*

'Sometimes you bark up the wrong tree. And sometimes you're in a different forest.' JAMES to MATTHEW, *The Apprentice*

32

'It's driving me mental already. All I want is a cigarette and I don't even fucking smoke.'
JAYNE MIDDLEMISS, *Celebrity Love Island*

'She's several sandwiches short of a picnic.'
CHRISTINE HAMILTON on TARA PALMER-TOMKINSON, *I'm a Celebrity ... Get Me Out of Here!*, Series 1

'I have been with a Cancerian woman for years. I can read their minds.' BEZ to BRIGITTE NIELSEN, whose star sign is Cancer, *Celebrity Big Brother*, Series 3

'I'm going nuts ... I'm fucking talking to myself ... This is the first sign of insanity.' TANIA to herself, *BB4*

'Something miraculous has happened. I've turned into a nice person.' JANET STREET-PORTER, *I'm a Celebrity ... Get Me Out of Here!*, Series 4

INSULT
NUMBER 20

'He's a Carebear gone wrong.'

SCIENCE on CRAIG, *BB6*

On Beauty ...

'You know what Rik Waller's body fat was?
Sixty per cent. I looked that up. That is the
same per cent fat as a pork scratching.'
RICKY GERVAIS on *Celebrity Fit Club*

'I was a skinny bird when I came in here,
but now my clothes are too thin for me.'
JADE, *BB3*

'I'm a beaten-up old Renault Clio and you've
got three months to turn me into a Ferrari!'
CRAIG CHARLES, *The Games*, Series 3

'It's not an issue.'
thirty-stone RIK
WALLER on his
weight, *Celebrity Fit
Club*, Series 1

'You are both the best-looking blokes in the house, removing me from the equation because that would be unfair.' PJ, *BB3*

SIMON COWELL: 'What's that show with Matt Lucas in it?'

LOUIS WALSH: '*Little Britain.*'

SIMON COWELL: 'Yes, Fiona, you look like that character in *Little Britain.*'

PAM: 'Vicky Pollard!'

FIONA: 'You mean I look like a man?'

SIMON COWELL: 'No, you don't look like a man, you look like a man who is dressed up as a woman.'

FIONA: 'A drag [queen]!'

SIMON COWELL to PAM: '. . . and you look like a stretched version of her.'

The two then went to The Pod to let out their frustrations.

FIONA: 'He wants to take a look in the mirror 'cause he's not all that.'

PAM: 'Ooh, I'd still do him, though.'

The X Factor, Series 1

'Cameron, could your legs be any whiter?! They look like Tippex.' LISA, *BB4*

'She's so ugly she could do an advert as a Twiglet.' JORDAN on JANET STREET-PORTER, *I'm a Celebrity . . . Get Me Out of Here!*, Series 4

'I don't need to be told I'm gorgeous, I know I am.' LESLEY, *BB3*

'She's had hair problems and her hair turned green and that's sad. I asked her, "Are you bald?" She said, "No, I've got some bits at the back."' PAUL DANAN on NIKKI ZIERING, *Celebrity Love Island*

'I did get the third most attractive glasses wearer [prize] in the *whole* of the UK *and* Holland.' ANOUSKA, *BB4*

'They have noses like pickaxes. You could cut stone with those noses.' SHARON OSBOURNE on SISTER MATIC, a couple of forty-one-year-old Bet Lynch lookalikes, *The X Factor*, Series 1

'You could hula-hoop through a Cheerio.' SCIENCE to KEMAL, *BB6*

'I look at the pictures and I don't recognise myself. It's nothing I am ashamed of, but my earrings were bigger than my tits.' JAYNE MIDDLEMISS on her topless photo shoot, *Celebrity Love Island*

'You look like an advert for WeightWatchers.' SIMON COWELL, *The X Factor*, Series 1

'I think of myself as an athlete because I have been on *Grandstand* and I wear trainers.' ANDY FORDHAM, *Celebrity Fit Club*, Series 3

PAUL: 'My wife never wears make-up. And if I met her and she was caked on with make-up, she would have missed the opportunity with me.'

BEN: 'She must be gutted.' *The Apprentice*

'I've got good hair, considering it's bleached. I'm a fake bird.' JADE, *BB3*

'I love your little pot belly.' PAUL DANAN to REBECCA LOOS, *Celebrity Love Island*

JAYNE MIDDLEMISS tells REBECCA LOOS about NIKKI ZIERING's special moisturiser made out of 'human foreskins' when PAUL DANAN declares, 'It's meant to be incredible for your face.'

JAYNE MIDDLEMISS: 'I don't know if I can put foreskin on my face.' *Celebrity Love Island*

'I am not ashamed or embarrassed to be a size 24 – I see myself as a glamorous chubbster!' AMY LAMÉ, *Celebrity Fit Club*, Series 2

'Nush is fit, but I don't know ... her toes are too long.' FEDERICO, *BB4*

'So Michael went off with an over-dressed, over-sized ... sorry over-sexed Abi Titmuss.' Presenter PATRICK KIELTY, *Celebrity Love Island*

'I used to be called "the whippet".' ANDY FORDHAM, *Celebrity Fit Club*, Series 3

'If I walked into a kitchen and saw someone who looks like he's auditioned for *Magnum PI*, they'd have to go ...They have got to come off.' GORDON RAMSAY on TOM VANCE's sunglasses, *Hell's Kitchen*, Series 1

'Geek chic.' KEMAL on EUGENE, *BB6*

'I used to be six foot four, you know, until a lift fell on me.' TONY BLACKBURN, *I'm a Celebrity . . . Get Me Out of Here!*, Series 1

'I've got really nice teeth . . . for someone who doesn't brush often.' SPENCER, *BB3*

ABI TITMUSS: 'I'm the cutest girl on the island.'
AUSSIE SURFER: 'I love English ladies, they're so funny.' *Celebrity Love Island*

'I look like a chip.' JUSTINE, *BB4*

'It's also very difficult, Sir Alan, particularly when you're in a party scenario like myself, to hear what people are saying when they are much lower down.' MATTHEW, *The Apprentice*

'I enjoyed not bathing, I enjoyed not changing my clothes.' TOYAH WILLCOX, *I'm a Celebrity ... Get Me Out of Here!*, Series 2

'Come with me, headscarf. Come with me now. Don't let me down, bitch.' KEMAL, *BB6*

KEN MORLEY: 'I want to look like you. Take my body and give me yours.'
DALE WINTON: 'That's a deal.' *Celebrity Fit Club*, Series 3

'I'm sitting here with three rolls of kebab hanging off.' JADE, *BB3*

'We're not telling you how you look! Do you want us to go there? Your hair looks like long pubic hair before a wax job!' CAPRICE to BRIGITTE NIELSEN, *Celebrity Big Brother*, Series 3

INSULT
NUMBER 19

'Dean, what people relate to
Paul? With all due respect,
they must be ten years of
age, love *Star Wars* and can
kick their legs really high.'

BRIAN, *BB2*

On Food and Cooking . . .

'I wouldn't serve that to my dog.'
GORDON RAMSAY on DWAIN
CHAMBERS's soufflé, *Hell's Kitchen*, Series 1

'What's in kidney beans?' HELEN, *BB2*

'I don't eat chicken's arse 'cos it's not good for
ya. D'ya get me?' SCIENCE, *BB6*

'Unhygienic? You've got a fucking hairnet on! It
won't make any difference for somebody so
fucking diseased!' GORDON RAMSAY to
EDWINA CURRIE, on her telling him he
was spitting while insulting her, *Hell's Kitchen*,
Series 1

'We're gonna be in here every day making pancakes, because the chickens lay them.' TANIA, *BB4*

'We can have fish shortbread.' SCOTT, *BB4*

'That's how I do mine in the morning.' AL MURRAY on blowtorching hair from pig's trotters, *Hell's Kitchen*, Series 1

'I hate sausages, they're such bitches.' CRAIG, *BB6*

'They pretty much taught us how to do everything you ever need to do to make posh food, which is basically cook it in butter, with too much salt.' AL MURRAY on pre-show training, *Hell's Kitchen*, Series 1

'How much chicken is there in chickpeas?' HELEN, *BB2*

'Edwina, you complain about cutting yourself and now you are shafting the restaurant like a sabotage mission.' GORDON RAMSAY to EDWINA CURRIE, *Hell's Kitchen*, Series 1

'What's asparagus? Do you grow it?' JADE, *BB3*

'Do I look as if I'm here to fucking cook you egg and chips?!' GORDON RAMSAY to VIC REEVES, *Hell's Kitchen*, Series 1

'I wouldn't know a coriander seed if it walked up and said hello.' JON, *BB4*

'I'm definitely the best cook in the world.'
ALISON, *BB3*

'How are you feeling, James? Because you look
like you are about to vomit.' GORDON
RAMSAY on making JAMES DREYFUS pluck
and behead pigeons, *Hell's Kitchen*, Series 1

'Kitchen scales! I need some of them.' BEZ on
what he could steal from the BB house.
Celebrity Big Brother, Series 3

'Strawberries and spuds.' JADE when asked
to name two vegetables from the BB garden,
BB3

'It's like sucking on a tramp's finger.' NUSH,
BB4

'I can't believe it, I didn't know how to boil an
egg.' JENNIFER ELLISON on winning *Hell's
Kitchen*, Series 1

49

'It was dead and it was in vodka – but it was pretty tasteless. It was really crunchy – I think it is probably quite a good source of protein.' ANTHONY WORRALL THOMPSON on eating scorpion before going on the show, *I'm a Celebrity . . . Get Me Out of Here!*, Series 2

'I've boiled an egg in the kettle hundreds of times – your tea doesn't taste that nice after it.' FEDERICO, *BB4*

'I worry about parsley . . . but I couldn't give a stuff about the fish.' JON, *BB4*

'I didn't do any [cooking]. It confirmed what I thought – kitchens are war zones. A chair attacked my leg today . . . and I banged into a cupboard once. My father never went into a kitchen – I never go into a kitchen.' JOHN McCRIRICK, *Celebrity Big Brother*, Series 3

INSULT
NUMBER 18

'Cellulite bitch.'

MICHELLE on VANESSA, *BB5*

On Science and Technology . . .

'I'm an ex-tractor fan.' KEITH HARRIS, *The Farm*, Series 1

'Menthol cigarettes make you infertile.' SOPHIE, *BB3*

'I know exactly how the world was formed.' JON, *BB4*

'I mean, she's got a Labradoodle, it's a biogenetic dog you order.' ABI TITMUSS on NIKKI ZIERING, *Celebrity Love Island*

'Ultra-violet radiation, nasty stuff.' JON, *BB4*

'Those infrared cameras can see under your duvet covers.' HELEN, *BB2*

INSULT
NUMBER 17

'Craig's head is so big it's got its own postcode.'

MAXWELL, *BB6*

On Politics . . .

'They were trying to use me as an escape goat.' JADE, *BB3*

'In the US we've got TWO sides – the Democrats and the Republicans. No other country can say that they have those!' VANILLA ICE, *The Farm*, Series 1

'One voting system which is always good for a laugh is the single transferable system.' EUGENE, *BB6*

'I think the hope for the future is William. King William and Queen Beyoncé.' PAUL BURRELL, *I'm a Celebrity . . . Get Me Out of Here!*, Series 4

'I feel like Churchill.' DEREK, *BB6*

'I've been shouted at by greater men and women than a thirty-seven-year-old cook.' EDWINA CURRIE on GORDON RAMSAY's chastising, *Hell's Kitchen*, Series 1

'Science is the first black man I've met who makes me want to join the BNP ... tomorrow.' DEREK, *BB6*

'I'll say what I like. 'Cos it's free speech, innit. D'ya get me?' SCIENCE, *BB6*

VANILLA ICE explained that he doesn't eat humous 'since they named a terrorist organisation after it' [presumably meaning Hamas], *The Farm*, Series 1

'I have been known as the Robert Kilroy-Silk of international diplomacy.' VICTOR, *BB5*

'The Union Jack is for all of us, but the St George is just for London, isn't it?' JADE, *BB3*

'You can't be a black person and be racist.' STAN COLLYMORE, *The Farm*, Series 1

'There's too much of that bombing shit going on.' LEE, *BB3*

'What is a Liberal Democrat?' HELEN, *BB2*

A bus pulled up outside the Manchester audition venue and TONY BLAIR stepped off. 'Are you auditioning today, Tony?' someone asked him. 'I'm auditioning all the time, mate, I tell you,' he replied. *The X Factor*, Series 1

INSULT
NUMBER 16

'Your head reminds me of a boiled egg.'

JADE, *BB3*

On the Finer Things in Life . . . The Arts

'Sandy. He was the horse from *Dogtanian* wasn't he? He's the only horse I know. *Dogtanian*. With the dogs.' ANTHONY, *BB6*

'I hate poems. I prefer being active and doing things, like flirting.' AHMED, *BB5*

'Books are good – it's like a magazine but it lasts longer.' STUART, *BB5*

'I think that's why art's so crap now, because artists are so poor.' NUSH, *BB4*

'Well, everybody died.' JON upon finishing a Shakespeare play, *BB4*

'There I was, my hair like God's gorilla.' JADE
[meaning Godzilla], *BB3*

INSULT
NUMBER 15

'I think Sandy was a boring old arsehole who had a big, massive, ten-foot cucumber up his fucking arse. He wouldn't know a good time if it shat all over his head.'

JONNY, *BB3*

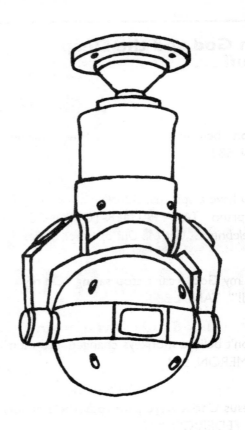

On God and the Deep Stuff . . .

'I don't believe in ghosts, but I've seen one.'
JON, *BB4*

'I do have a spiritual side. I've always played
the piano.' TARA PALMER-TOMKINSON, *I'm
a Celebrity . . . Get Me Out of Here!*, Series 1

'Oh my God! I can't stop saying, "Oh my
God!"' TANIA, *BB4*

'I don't believe monkeys changed into men.'
CAMERON, *BB4*

'If Jesus Christ were alive today, he'd be locked
up.' FEDERICO, *BB4*

'I put on my Star of David for you.'
PAUL DANAN to NIKKI ZIERING, *Celebrity Love Island*

'God, you've got to help me. Please make sure it's me tomorrow. I don't ask for your help often and I'm sorry I'm asking now, but you've got to help me.' TANIA, *BB4*

INSULT
NUMBER 14

'You wouldn't notice the smell, it wouldn't smell any worse than when he was alive.'

SCOTT while discussing what would happen if GOS died in bed, *BB4*

Some Things are Just Common Sense . . .

'I dreamt last night when I was asleep.'
HELEN, *BB2*

'I'll never wear a G-string in the jungle again.'
SOPHIE ANDERTON, *I'm a Celebrity . . . Get Me Out of Here!*, Series 4

'The thing is, Ray, what you've got to remember is that there are cameras behind the mirrors.' CAMERON, *BB4*

'I've got white marks under there [pointing at eyes] because I wore sunglasses. A couple of days before I came in here I got a sunbed and fell asleep with the goggles on, and since I've been getting more of a tan I haven't got rid of it and it just looks completely stupid.' PAUL DANAN, *Celebrity Love Island*

'If there wasn't any cigarettes, then I wouldn't smoke them.' TANIA, *BB4*

'It's a film.' VANILLA ICE in a game of charades, *The Farm*, Series 1

'Sleep is a wonderful thing. Time just passes ..' CAMERON, *BB4*

'When Glenn Hoddle was manager of Tottenham, apparently, in the middle of the night his phone rang and it was the Tottenham fire brigade and they said, "Mr Hoddle, there's terrible news. There's a massive fire at White Hart Lane and it's serious." "Oh my gosh! The cups! We've gotta save the cups!" "It's all right Mr Hoddle. The fire hasn't reached the canteen yet."' PAUL, *The Apprentice*

'The sun is still there. It's just covered with loads of clouds and things.' SCOTT, *BB4*

'Dressed? What, as in clothes?' HELEN, *BB2*

'Excuse me. What is the protocol on having a leech?' JOE PASQUALE, *I'm a Celebrity ... Get Me Out of Here!*, Series 4

'I can see you on the radio.' TANIA, *BB4*

'If there were less people in here, it would be less crowded.' DEAN, *BB2*

'I feel it's the right choice at the right time, and because you're so not the right man for the job.' RICHIE NEVILLE on electing VANILLA ICE as farm leader, *The Farm*, Series 1

'We bought the pre-packed flowers for £2.25 and we sold them for £1.60.' MIRANDA, *The Apprentice*

'I'm either staying or going tonight.' STUART on eviction night, *BB5*

INSULT
NUMBER 13

'There is more mince in that walk than there is in the freezer.'

DEREK on KEMAL, *BB6*

Speaking While Under the Influence . . .

'God save vodka.' RAY, *BB4*

'[If I ruled the world] I'd decrease the cost of beer and make girls a lot looser.' PJ, *BB3*

'I won't be able to stop the drinking just like that, but I've hopefully cut it in half, and if you cut what I drink in half that is a hell of a lot.' ANDY FORDHAM, *Celebrity Fit Club*, Series 3

'I could drink White Lightening out of a champagne glass and it would taste the same.' STEPH, *BB4*

'I like to get drunk and make a fool of myself.'
JADE, *BB3*

'It gets to me when people act like the world's going to end if they don't get another glass of alcohol.' LADY ISABELLA HERVEY, *Celebrity Love Island*

'They say alcohol gives you a loose tongue, but when I get drunk I usually get my baps out.'
LISA, *BB4*

INSULT
NUMBER 12

'Roberto is inconsiderate, in-sensitive, there's an endless list – backwards: a cock, a dick, annoying, horrible, nasty, a bully, intimidating, over the top, under the top, around the top. And I'm punking that bitch by nominating him now.'

KEMAL, *BB6*

Education and the Three 'R's

'God! How come you lot have got loads and I have only got two.' HELEN on GCSEs, *BB2*

'Paul, have you read a book in the past six months not based on a film or a TV series and that isn't a pot-boiler?' JANET STREET-PORTER, *I'm a Celebrity ... Get Me Out of Here!*, Series 4

'Yeah, one million per cent, one million per cent.' SASKIA, *BB6*

'We don't have fucking double "l"s and double "o"s in Portuguese . . . fucking double "l"s, it's not fair.' NADIA on failing a spelling test, *BB5*

'Her time would be better spent having four years learning the alphabet.' VICTOR on EMMA, *BB5*

'I told Big Brother so many things you've learnt me, and I've been proud.' JADE to ALEX, *BB3*

'Don't push me too far because I am very fucking articulate.' RHONA CAMERON, *I'm a Celebrity . . . Get Me Out of Here!*, Series 1

'I am intelligent, but I let myself down because I can't speak properly or spell.' JADE, *BB3*

'I chose French. I got an F.' STEPH, *BB4*

'I could learn a random language, Hebrew or something.' TIM, *BB3*

'Do they speak Portuganese in Portugal? I thought Portugal was in Spain.' JADE, *BB3*

INSULT
NUMBER 11

'I might as well talk to my arse; I'd get a better response.'

JAYNE MIDDLEMISS on LEE SHARPE, *Celebrity Love Island*

Family Values . . .

'I've got the biggest boobs in Huddersfield.
Well, apart from me mum and me nan.'
LESLEY, *BB6*

'I feel bad now, Shell just asked me if I can
have children or not. I will have to invent a
story but I do not want to lie.' NADIA, *BB5*

'Edwina was always a pleasure – it is just
like cooking next to your mum all day
long.' GORDON RAMSAY, *Hell's Kitchen*,
Series 1

'I treat my mum as a mum, and she treats me
as a daughter.' JADE, *BB3*

'My mum wants me to become a stripper.'
LEE, *BB3*

'I like looking after people and animals. I always do my mum's make-up and pluck her eyebrows.' LYNNE, *BB3*

'I just want my mum.' SOPHIE, *BB3*

MAKOSI: 'My mother was one of fifty children.'
SCIENCE: 'Your grandaddy was a pimp.' *BB3*

'I want my mummy ... I'm going to be sick.' NATALIE APPLETON, *I'm a Celebrity ... Get Me Out of Here!*, Series 4

'I've got more pictures of my car than I've got of my family, I think.' GOS, *BB4*

'What am I going to call my baby? "Big Brother Jacuzzi?"' MAKOSI, *BB6*

'Yes, I am from the ghetto. Yes, I live with my mum.' SCIENCE, *BB6*

'You can't not put me through! My mum will go mad.' ROWETTA, *The X Factor*, Series 1

INSULT
NUMBER 10

'She's up her own fucking tits.'

PAUL DANAN on ABI TITMUSS,
Celebrity Love Island

On Nature and Stuff ...

'I can't help it if I don't know what "metalabism" is.' JADE, *BB3*

'Oh my God! I touched a tree!' NATALIE APPLETON, *I'm a Celebrity ... Get Me Out of Here!*, Series 4

PAUL DANAN killing a fish he's caught for LADY ISABELLA HERVEY:
'Oh God, he's not moving! Oh Goddd! You can make it! Ohhhhhhhhh Godddddddddddddd!!!!!' *Celebrity Love Island*

'I want people to see I can get my hands dirty. In fact there is nothing I like more than covering myself in mud.' TARA PALMER-TOMKINSON, *I'm a Celebrity ... Get Me Out of Here!*, Series 1

'Man, I know what ma DNA stands for – Dis Negro is Attractive aiiiiight.' VICTOR, *BB5*

'I have never in my whole life touched a worm.' TARA PALMER-TOMKINSON, *I'm a Celebrity ... Get Me Out of Here!*, Series 1

'Did you get stuck to the toilet seat?' BRIGITTE NIELSEN to KENZIE, who had a 'tummy bug', *Celebrity Big Brother*, Series 3

'Sometimes Uri dramatises little things like farts like he's an alien who's never heard one before.' RHONA CAMERON, *I'm a Celebrity ... Get Me Out of Here!*, Series 1

PAUL DANAN: 'I could balance this whole duvet [on my manhood].'
ABI TITMUSS: 'Don't flatter yourself ... I think you are being a bit optimistic there.'
Celebrity Love Island

'There is such a thing as colon cancer, I just can't think where your colon is.' TANIA, *BB4*

'It's called a condom?' URI GELLER on a quandong, a local fruit, *I'm a Celebrity ... Get Me Out of Here!*, Series 1

'If you chopped my head off, I'd still carry on talking, 'cos the head stays alive for a bit.' JADE to JAMES HEWITT, *Back to Reality*

'There's a spider on my bed. Please can you come and get it? Please somebody.' NATALIE APPLETON, *I'm a Celebrity ... Get Me Out of Here!*, Series 4

'I saw these huge white underwear and then I just felt the wind and the smell, and it was miserable.' BRIGITTE NIELSEN, on JOHN McCRIRICK, *Celebrity Big Brother*, Series 3

'One night, two rats the size of Jack Russells were shagging on my forehead – and another one went into my sleeping bag.' TARA PALMER-TOMKINSON, *I'm a Celebrity . . . Get Me Out of Here!*, Series I

'Oh my Gawd, there go the chickens. Chow mein!!!!!' VANILLA ICE, *The Farm*, Series I

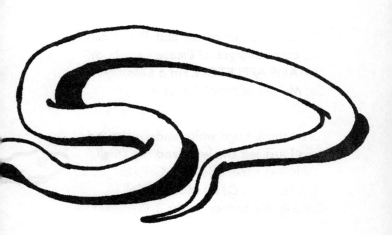

INSULT
NUMBER 9

'Your ass looks like two elephants wrestling.'

JONNY, *BB3*

On Music . . .

'What is a music man without his music?'
PETER ANDRE, *I'm a Celebrity . . . Get Me Out
of Here!*, Series 3

'Singing involves giving pleasure – you can't.
You also look like you've been dragged
through a bush.' SIMON COWELL, *Pop Idol*

'In the olden days they had wirelophones and
they got music out of that.' JADE, *BB3*

'I've written this song called *Insania* – it's a mix
of "insane" and "mania", and even though it's a
made-up word, you instantly know what it
means!' PETER ANDRE, *I'm a Celebrity . . . Get
Me Out of Here!*, Series 3

LOUIS WALSH: 'I think you're more Shakin'
   Stevens than Elvis Presley,'
SIMON COWELL 'Hmm. I think you're more
   Shufflin' Stevens than Shakin' Stevens.'
The X Factor, Series 1

'My advice would be: if you want to pursue a career in the music business, don't.' SIMON COWELL, *Pop Idol*

'I think a quaver is a cheesy crisp.' FEDERICO, *BB4*

INSULT
NUMBER 8

'If I wanted to hear an arsehole, I would just fart.'

RON JEREMY to KEITH HARRIS,
The Farm, Series 2

On Manners and Etiquette . . .

'Well, I don't barge into other conversations, and I would be grateful if you didn't barge into mine!' DEREK, *BB6*

'At the time it was a better option than sucking your fingers or licking oil out of your butt crack.' NUSH on licking her nipple, *BB4*

'Come on everybody, let's wipe our bums on the wall if we haven't got any loo roll.' NUSH, *BB4*

'I was expecting you to smell. People told me you would, but you don't.' JADE to RIK WALLER, *Back to Reality*

'There are going to be noises coming from my arse tonight.' SCOTT, *BB4*

'I don't understand that whole mentality of reading books on the toilet.' STEPH, *BB4*

'It's hideous even to watch them eat. Rather like the English language, they haven't perfected the art of eating, either.' DEREK, *BB6*

'I'm sorry that I'm very, very loud but I was born with this gob and I've got to use it.'
SAIRA, *The Apprentice*

'Don't no one go near my bed 'cos I've been doing rancids.' TANIA, *BB4*

'Jonny told me it was normal to piss in the shower and I felt like saying, "Well, I'll come round to your house and piss in your shower, then."' ALEX, *BB3*

'A cummerbund plays havoc with trying to pull a moony.' JONNY, *BB3*

INSULT
NUMBER 7

'Does it bother you that you have tiny, tiny breasts?'

URI GELLER to TARA PALMER-TOMKINSON, *I'm a Celebrity . . . Get Me Out of Here,* Series 1

baby
Oil

Mister Bingo
14 FL OZ (414ml)

Love and Sex . . .

JOSH: 'I've had four wet dreams . . . I wake up
in the morning covered.'
HELEN: 'Covered in what?' *BB2*

'Do I have to have sex? All right, I'll do it for
Britain. I'll think of England.' ABI TITMUSS,
Celebrity Love Island

'If I had an offer I'd have been married by now.'
TANIA, *BB4*

'He's lovely and I think the world of Paul, but if
you want to win a girl round, you don't get a
blowy in a bog off someone else.' JAYNE
MIDDLEMISS, *Celebrity Love Island*

101

'I was born with two virginities, but I've still got a third to lose.' KEMAL, *BB6*

'Do you always two-time people, Edwina? First you're shagging a prime minister, and now you're shagging me up the arse from behind.' GORDON RAMSAY, *Hell's Kitchen*, Series 1

'I'm a virgin.' MAKOSI, *BB6*

'I'm not a virgin.' MAKOSI, *BB6*

'[He's] fucking on the toilet ... does it not bother any of you?" STAN COLLYMORE on VANILLA ICE, *The Farm*, Series 1

ABI TITMUSS: 'My tit was out!'
LEE SHARPE: 'I didn't even notice.'
ABI TITMUSS: 'That's fantastic. My boob was out and you were looking at my face; that's a novelty.' *Celebrity Love Island*

'I like a man to bark like a dog.' SASKIA, *BB6*

'Callum's getting bored of her now because she farts and she's a lesbian.' PAUL DANAN on CALLUM BEST and REBECCA LOOS, *Celebrity Love Island*

'Most men don't mind good-looking lesbians.' VICTOR, *BB5*

TARA PALMER-TOMKINSON: 'It's like deprivation. You can get quite uptight if you can't. I'm just fucking horned up. I think that is because I'm very highly sexed.'
DARREN DAY: 'Tara, can I ask you something? Why didn't you tell me this four years ago?'
I'm a Celebrity . . . Get Me Out of Here!, Series 1

'Imagine marrying someone and finding out that they're hung like a mosquito.' ABI TITMUSS, *Celebrity Love Island*

'I've no idea if I'm good in bed because I've never slept with the same girl twice, you don't get the feedback.' JON, *BB4*

'We did not have sex ... it was just a bit of a fumble.' SASKIA, *BB6*

'I've always been a major sex symbol. This is the problem that I have.' TONY BLACKBURN, *I'm a Celebrity ... Get Me Out of Here!*, Series 1

'You will find someone with a screwdriver who will open your heart.' MICHAEL GRECO to FRAN COSGROVE, *Celebrity Love Island*

'I'm the horniest man in the world.' PJ, *BB3*

'At the end of the day I like women and I've got a lot of love to give!' PAUL DANAN, *Celebrity Love Island*

'You don't know, I'm a fucking animal, and that's without Viagra.' LEE, *BB3*

'I don't see the point in snogging someone unless you want to shag them.' SPENCER, *BB3*

'You smell nice. You don't mind if I smoke, do you?' FRAN COSGROVE to JAYNE MIDDLEMISS, *Celebrity Love Island*

'I'd love to be seen as a sex object.' JONNY, *BB3*

'You can be the bitch in the relationship.' RAY to CAMERON, *BB4*

'It's not easy being a bisexual.' REBECCA LOOS, *Celebrity Love Island*

'If you want something to suck on, just ask me.' RAY, *BB4*

'I'd love it if you'd smack me.' REBECCA LOOS to CALLUM BEST, *Celebrity Love Island*

'I'm so happy tonight, I could sleep with a woman.' DEREK, *BB6*

'Are you going to have to have a tommy tank?' REBECCA LOOS to CALLUM BEST, *Celebrity Love Island*

'I just want a big man with rough hands to slap me or something.' NADIA, *BB5*

'She loves it.' PAUL DANAN on ABI TITMUSS, *Celebrity Love Island*

'Does he work on women?' MIKEY GREEN on Gwyn the sheepdog's herding skills, *The Farm*, Series 2

'My mum said, "So what if you had an orgy? If it was Roman times, nobody would bat an eyelid!"' ABI TITMUSS, *Celebrity Love Island*

'Jade, can you please take your eyes somewhere else? She's looking at my package!' ALEX, *BB3*

'I think I've been giving him massive signals. Short of tattooing "I fancy you" across my head.' JAYNE MIDDLEMISS on LEE SHARPE, *Celebrity Love Island*

'I can see the press now ... Tony Blackburn left alone in the jungle with four women. At least they'll be safe.' TONY BLACKBURN, *I'm a Celebrity ... Get Me Out of Here!*, Series 1

'I've admitted I like him, it's not good for anyone. I don't even support Man United.' JAYNE MIDDLEMISS on LEE SHARPE, *Celebrity Love Island*

'Your hormones are going crackers. There's an earthquake in your nether regions.' JONNY on LEE and SOPHIE, *BB3*

'It makes me want sex. Oh my God, it's like sex!' LIZ McCLARNON on chocolate mousse, *Celebrity Love Island*

SOPHIE ANDERTON: 'Nothing can be more revolting than having a testicle in your mouth.' FRAN COSGROVE: 'It's gotta take some balls to eat some balls.' *I'm a Celebrity . . . Get Me Out of Here!*, Series 4

'I wouldn't even fit in a toilet cubicle, let alone mash someone up against the wall.' FRAN COSGROVE on the perils of mile-high nookie, *Celebrity Love Island*

DAVINA McCALL: 'What's it like living with
    Caprice?'
KENZIE: 'Nice, to wake up in the morning.
    Special!' *Celebrity Big Brother*, Series 3

'Being a love rat, I'm used to the smell of the
sewers.' DARREN DAY, *I'm a Celebrity ... Get
Me Out of Here!*, Series 1

'I'm not expecting to see her fully blown when
I get home.' LEE SHARPE on ABI TITMUSS,
Celebrity Love Island

'From my experience I've never had a lesbian
experience.' STEPH, *BB4*

'You never wear very many clothes. Do you
ever get cold?' ANT and DEC interviewing
JORDAN, *I'm a Celebrity ... Get Me Out of
Here!*, Series 3

'Shall we not play Spin the Bottle and just tongue each other?' NUSH, *BB4*

'My nightmare was a vision of her [Edwina Currie] in the nude.' GORDON RAMSAY, *Hell's Kitchen*, Series 1

REBECCA LOOS on pleasuring a pig: 'My arms are aching! It lasts for about ten minutes and he starts thrusting really hard and then I grip!'
STAN COLLYMORE: 'Was it good? Did you feel it?' *The Farm*, Series 1

'We don't go to bed late or masturbate/ The camera's always there but that's our fate.' PAUL DANAN tries his hand at songwriting, *Celebrity Love Island*

'I don't perve on you. But if I see you in a pair of tight boxer shorts ...' CRAIG to ANTHONY, *BB6*

INSULT
NUMBER 6

'For those of you not familiar
with surfer speak, "stoked"
means happy, a "breaker" is a
wave, and a "Titmuss" is a
slapper.'

Presenter PATRICK KIELTY, *Celebrity
Love Island*

Hobbies Maketh the Man ...

'I love blinking I do.' HELEN, *BB2*

'I could kill somebody with these two fingers.'
LISA, *BB4*

'I love birds ... I used to wash my budgie once
a week in washing-up liquid.' DARREN, *BB1*

INSULT
NUMBER 5

'Derek is a little man bitch.'

KEMAL, *BB6*

On Geography ...

'Have they not got seasides in Birmingham?'
JADE, *BB3*

'I had an English boyfriend in high school, but
he didn't have the accent. His father did and I
thought he was adorable.' NIKKI ZIERING,
Celebrity Love Island

'I wouldn't move to Redditch, absolutely not
... no matter who lived there ... Steph or
Demi Moore.' CAMERON, *BB4*

'I'm not walking in Tottenham.' TIM, *The
Apprentice*

'Rio de Janeiro, ain't that a person?' JADE, *BB3*

'Saskia told me what the ghetto was earlier. I thought it was a country.' CRAIG, *BB6*

'I love Real Madrid. I could watch Italian football all day.' JAYNE MIDDLEMISS trying to chat up LEE SHARPE, *Celebrity Love Island*

'If you look like your passport photo, you're too ill to travel.' JOE PASQUALE, *I'm a Celebrity . . . Get Me Out of Here!*, Series 4

'We get terrible problems with wasps . . . and there's squirrels everywhere.' JON on Staines, *BB4*

'Did you know that you would need 179,728 Fruit and Nut bars to stretch the length of Bermuda? I could eat it in five days.' KATE, *BB3*

'I've been to Japan. I went to Tokyo. Konnichiwa. Konnichiwa. You remember?' SAIRA to a Japanese woman, *The Apprentice*

'I knew Lynne was from Aberdeen but I didn't realise Aberdeen was in Scotland.' JADE, *BB3*

INSULT NUMBER 4

'I may be known as the girl who was sunbathing topless with a prince, but Jordan is known as that thick girl who always falls out of clubs drunk. I know which one I prefer.'

JENNY FROST, *I'm a Celebrity . . . Get Me Out of Here,* Series 3

On Pets and Fowl Crushes . . .

'This is awful. I feel like I'm sending pigs to a concentration camp.' DEBBIE McGEE, *The Farm*, Series 1

'Look at the funny little monkey. It's laughing at me. Oh look, it's so sweet.' DEREK, *BB6*

'Mr Moth, I respect your wishes. You don't move for no one.' SCIENCE, *BB6*

'That's what ducks eat!' JEFF BRAZIER on a duck not eating the croissant he had given it, *The Farm*, Series 1

'Doesn't look like a chicken, does he? Looks like a bird.' STEPH, *BB4*

121

'I'll never see them chickens again. It's the closest thing I've ever had to a pet. I'm gonna nick a Polaroid of them. I like those chickens, I really do.' ALEX, *BB3*

'Just give them a little slap.' FARMER RYAN to STAN COLLYMORE on herding stubborn cows, *The Farm*, Series 1

'[It says here] chickens are used to being free-range and independent . . . so why can't they clean their own house, then?' GOS, *BB4*

'I'll definitely miss the emus when I'm gone.' JOE PASQUALE, *I'm a Celebrity . . . Get Me Out of Here!*, Series 4

'Stella is the archetypical common chicken.' NUSH, *BB4*

'If I'm drunk one night I'm gonna fucking kill one of those chickens.' FEDERICO, *BB4*

'Don't forget that I want a donkey filled with sweets.' ANNA, *BB1*

'I think Matilda is beautiful.' FEDERICO, *BB4*

'I used to hate Black Beauty. If I'd have had a machine gun, I'd have killed that horse ... Black Beauty, Lassie and all the kids from "Grandma, We Love You" ... in one hit, man.' GOS, *BB4*

JADE: 'I think them chickens have given me
    fleas.'
JONNY: 'Maybe you gave the chickens fleas.'
    BB3

INSULT
NUMBER 3

'Just go ahead and roll out of
here like you rolled in here, you
great big wide whale.'

Trainer HARVEY to AMY LAMÉ,
Celebrity Fit Club, Series 2

On Class . . .

'Rich people are always gonna have horses.'
JON, *BB4*

'Tony, before I came in here – I've got to tell you – I don't think I've ever done my own washing in my life – I don't think I've practically ever made my own bed. I'll admit it.'
TARA PALMER-TOMKINSON, *I'm a Celebrity . . . Get Me Out of Here!*, Series 1

'You're a gentleman . . . is this all a little bit lairy?' NUSH to CAMERON, *BB4*

'I'd be the most common queen in the world!'
KERRY McFADDEN, *I'm a Celebrity . . . Get Me Out of Here!*, Series 3

126

'No, Roberto, let him cook the chicken like the peasant he is.' DEREK about SCIENCE, *BB6*

'Contrary to the belief of the nation I am far from being a snob.' TARA PALMER-TOMKINSON, *I'm a Celebrity ... Get Me Out of Here!*, Series 1

'Me dad said to me, "You'll last four weeks at the most because of your accent." He reckoned a lot of people down south wouldn't understand us.' JONNY, *BB3*

'I caught her [Queen Elizabeth] once in her sitting room wearing the imperial crown ... She was practising wearing it for the Opening of Parliament. She was sat with her crown on and her pink fluffy slippers.' PAUL BURRELL, *I'm a Celebrity ... Get Me Out of Here!*, Series 4

'I don't live in a hood, I live in a cul-de-sac.' CRAIG, *BB6*

'I will try to be myself and it should bring a different perspective, a different level of society, I suppose.' TIM, *BB3*

'I'm a double-barrelled woman with three houses.' JANET STREET-PORTER, *I'm a Celebrity ... Get Me Out of Here!*, Series 4

'He's fucking common as muck!' PENNY on
BUBBLE, *BB2*

'We should all stick together because we're all
from the street.' DARREN DAY on friendship
with TARA PALMER-TOMKINSON and
NIGEL BENN, *I'm a Celebrity . . . Get Me Out of
Here!*, Series 1

'Have you been sworded?' JADE to JAMES
HEWITT [meaning, presumably, knighted],
Back to Reality

INSULT
NUMBER 2

'She's a big fat slag and I
want to crunch her face in.'

JAYNE MIDDLEMISS (small)

TITMUSS, Celebrity Love Island

INSULT
NUMBER 2

'She's a big fat slag and I want to crunch her face in.'

JAYNE MIDDLEMISS on ABI TITMUSS, *Celebrity Love Island*

Confucius Didn't Say . . .

'How can we ration when people aren't being rational?' SCIENCE, *BB6*

'Swans who carry knives, now they're dangerous.' SCOTT, *BB4*

'It would be great if whales could fly.' NUSH, *BB4*

'How come you chop a tree down, then you chop it up?' PETER ANDRE, *I'm a Celebrity . . . Get Me Out of Here!*, Series 3

'Everyone's like the same, but everyone's different, do you know what I mean?' TANIA, *BB4*

'Dreams are roads to the inner consciousness.'
STUART, *BB5*

'I've got to be a big strong boy today, use
every bit of strength in me.' TIM, *BB3*

'I love the idea of being a glamour model.'
MICHELLE, *BB5*

'Our fate's in the hands of fluffy animals.'
SCOTT, *BB4*

'I don't lead a complex life, all I want is fags.'
SPENCER, *BB3*

'The best thing you can give someone is your
laughter.' GOS, *BB4*

'I wish everything was just nice.' NUSH, *BB4*

'I still like to expect the worst.' ALEX, *BB3*

'Being sick ain't pleasant, remember.' SCOTT, *BB4*

'Oh, we do get ourselves into some pickles in life, don't we?' STEPH, *BB4*

'The world is not right. Brian McFadden's left Westlife – it's going to take me ages to get over that.' VICTOR, *BB5*

'We should live life and snog as many people as we can.' PAUL DANAN, *Celebrity Love Island*

'Opinions are like arseholes, everyone's got one.' SCOTT, *BB4*

AND
INSULT
NUMBER 1...

'You're a waste of sperm.'

Trainer HARVEY to RIK WALLER,
Celebrity Fit Club, Series 1

Acknowledgements

Thanks must go firstly to the contestants, without whom such a funny tome would not be possible. Thanks must also go to Lorraine Baxter, Charlotte Clerk, Helen Ewing, Ellie Fry, Laura Collins, Laura Mell, Laura Morris, Stephanie Oliver and Mr Bingo for helping to create such a great book from other people's clangers.